Adapting Resiliently

A healing journey to vitality by address inflammation mind,

body and spirit.

Aubrey Mast, MPH

PhD Candidate Mind Body Medicine

www.adaptingresiliently.com

2021

Dedication

To all those that feel the call to be bigger, brighter and more

enthusiastically alive.

I am grateful for the love of many, the wind to my cheeks,

the sound of jazz in my ears, the sight of blooming flowers

and the feeling of unadulterated earth beneath my feet.

Thank you to my parents for bringing me in, for my son for

awakening me, and my sacred circle people for your ongoing

support.

I am honored to be in this life with you.

"To change one's life:

1. Start immediately.

2. Do it flamboyantly.

3. No exceptions."

William James

Table of Contents

Introduction

When you hear the word inflammation, what do you think of? For me, I think of things (typically cuts or cells) becoming red hot, swollen, visibly agitated and in discomfort. Travel with me for a second, what if inflammation was not only reserved to the concept of cuts and cells. What if, we could take the broadest sense of this term; hot, agitated in discomfort and we applied it to all dimensions of wellness. All the sudden, we can see that we can become inflamed in a multitude of ways. Inflammation is a term that's throw around pretty widely these days, typically it pertains to the physical body. In this book I will be exploring the concept of inflammation as it relates to agitation, heat, discomfort within our mental, emotional, physical, nutritional, spiritual and social determinants of health.

The most common approach to inflammation is an understanding of what happens within the physical body. Inflammation in isolated events is essential to health and wellbeing. We fall down and we get a cut, then the body releases inflammatory markers to cue the bleeding to stop, a scab to protect the cut so that the cut can heal while the inflammation helps to protect against infection. In this case, inflammation is a good thing. However, when we have chronic exposure to inflammation, it stops being good for us and instead becomes dangerous. We will explore inflammatory markers that are related with disease processes and even prevention. The prevention of most diseases and illnesses often lies in reducing the amount of chronic exposure to inflammation. These inflammatory markers can be exasperated by lifestyle choices.

For our time together, let's assume that inflammation is related to stress. Let's consider that we experience stress mentally, emotionally, physically, nutritionally, socially and spiritually. Inflammation is stress

6

bodies. During our time together we will gain an understanding of what the research is saying about inflammation in all of these realms. The reality is that when we talk about adapting resiliently what we are really discussing is how to decrease inflammation by better equipping ourselves to respond to mental, emotional, nutrition, physical and social stressors. When we are better able to respond and react then the inflammation does not get out of hand. We are then able to make lifestyle choices that are impactful to mind-body-spirit and aid in stepping into our sovereignty and optimal wellbeing.

This book seeks to understand what inflammation looks like in each arena of holistic wellbeing. We will explore what the research is showing about the characteristics of inflammation in each of these dimensions. Also, we will learn how to neutralize the inflammation and stress through tools that increase self-efficacy and actualization, allowing us to adapt to stressors with a greater sense of resiliency.

Towards the end of the book, we will look at resiliency practices. These practices can be used in solidarity or as a guide towards making holistic lifestyle changes. In the face of inflammation, it is important to consider which area is asking for your attention the most at this time. From there, it is important to grasp that all areas of holistic wellbeing are interrelated. You may be called to explore nutritional inflammation within the gut only to find that it helps ease stress and inflammation in your mind. What you do on one level you are doing on all.

I believe that we all deserve to live of life of vibrant health. In all of my years studying health, I have come to realize that inflammation in the broadest sense of the word is the determinant that keeps us from optimal functioning. Adapting Resiliently is my attempt to bridge the research and understanding of ways in which we can reduce stress and inflammation and in turn step into lives that have us feeling healthful, vibrant, connected and sovereign.

Physical Inflammation

For me the avenue towards my sacred self-began with a health crisis. Here we are discussing physical inflammation and you may be wondering how a health crisis could connect with the spiritual and sacred self. It is my hope throughout the next chapters of where and how inflammation manifests itself, you are able to see that one area of wellness impacts all. All are one and all are interconnected.

I was in not the best relationships; those where you completely discount yourself, where you turn off the inner knowing and somehow convince yourself that all you are aware of is not true. The result of this kind of relationship for me looked like eating acidic (processed + fast) foods, not sleeping, smoking cigarettes, quitting all of my creative endeavors, having reactive outbursts and frequently ignoring my thoughts and emotions. I was a mess to say the least. This went on for months if not years. I had many spiritual

9

cues that I wasn't in alignment with my soul's journey. I had wandered off course to learn valuable lessons of being redirected back towards myself. It's funny how spirit works like that, even when you make choices that deep down you know you should do differently, eventually you are course corrected no matter how you feel life should go.

The accumulation of stress got the best of me. My physical body is my barometer for when I have traveled off of my sacred course, I have symptoms that appear to get my attention about what kind of healing needs to take place. In this case it responded in grand magnitude, I had stopped paying attention to all the areas of inflammation in my life. The result was that I was in and out of hospitals, without a clear clue on what was going on, only to find out that my ovaries had veins around them that weren't pumping blood to my heart and would instead rub on my ovary (painfully) to get my attention.

Let's just take this moment to zoom out of what I just described into a more intuitive based perspective. The ovaries store life creation. Our veins carry nutrients and life force energy throughout our bodies. My body was telling me that my life force energy was getting stopped up on my lack of honoring what I was here to create (big surprise- I am not here to create a life where I discount my intuition and go against my highest knowing and worth). (Neither are you!) This marked the beginning of my life's journey towards a life of vitality, healing and sacred living. My story began with my body demanding alkalinity and balance which just so happened to shift all the other areas (one by one) towards balance.

In this chapter we will explore how physical inflammation and stress showcases itself. We will look at symptoms of physical inflammation and then explore how nutrition can contribute to the inflammation felt in our body.

Symptoms

We all experience stress differently just like we all have various stressors. Physical symptoms of stress can include aches, pains, diarrhea, constipation, nausea, dizziness, chest pain, diarrhea, constipation, loss of sex drive, rapid heartbeat, and frequent colds (Bigham et.al., 2014). We may experience these symptoms of stress in isolated events or they may become continuous experiences. Stress showcases itself to us in the physical form so that we may be presented with an awareness of something that is happening which is causing distress. This distress can happen not only physically but also mentally, emotionally, spiritually and socially. We can equally experience these physical symptoms of stress because of any of those areas of wellbeing being unbalanced, especially when the presence of lived stressors is chronic. The physical symptoms and exposure to stress can trigger an inflammatory response in protection to the body. We respond to stress, no matter the type. Our body releases inflammatory markers to signal a physiological response.

Inflammatory Markers

When my body was in pain, or I chose nutrient depleted inflammatory foods, or I got into an argument; I felt that emotionally and mentally as well as physically. In response my body would releases a cascade of inflammatory markers to signal the need to respond to some kind of stressor.

When we experience stress or a traumatic event (no matter how 'big' or 'small') we release inflammatory markers. Remember, the true purpose of inflammatory markers is to help protect us against foreign invaders. We can release inflammatory markers that can be detected via cells, blood, organs, gastro-intestinally, neurologically as well as through our breath, saliva, and sweat.

Systematic and chronic inflammation is often measured by analyzing varying inflammatory markers. These markers can include acute-phase proteins, pro-inflammatory cytokines (Il-6), natural killer cells (NK cells), C-reactive

13

protein (CRP), and white blood cells (WBC) (Speer et al.,

2018, p 111). Inflammatory markers can also include

erythrocyte sedimentation rate (ESR) and plasma viscosity

(PV) (Watson, et. al., (2019). We are also able to express

adrenaline through our sweat, cortisol through our saliva

and exhale nitric oxide.

Individual and chronic responses to stressors can

produce varying levels of detectable inflammatory markers.

Chronic low-grade inflammation has also shown changes to

the pro-inflammatory cytokines, interleukin-6 (IL-6), tumor

necrosis factor (TNF), and IL-1 (Speer et al., 2018, p 112).

Remember, cytokines are the substances released in the

body which impact cellular function. Interleukin-6 (IL-6), C-

Reactive protein (CRP), and tumor necrosis factor (TNF) are

common inflammatory markers monitored for their

relationship with heart disease, cancer, diabetes, dementia,

and depression among others. Erythrocyte sedimentation

rate (ESR) and plasma viscosity (PV) are measured for their

participation in inflammatory conditions, infections, auto-immune conditions and cancers (Watson, et. al., (2019).

When I saw what was going on with my body, I was able to make a decision of how I wanted to respond. I went forward taking medications and trying the allopathic model. Ultimately it did not help my inflammation and often brought greater complications. I also explored more holistic modalities. With the holistic practitioners I was asking myself about my sleep, emotional habits, relationships, sources of fun, work, and personal habits alongside with the physical ailments of my condition. What I learned through these encounters was that I was experiencing a call towards healing. After dealing with hospitalizations, multiples practitioners, the strain upon my relationships and my ability to work or engage with others, I learned that if I wanted to feel, respond, be treated, or have access to something different it would require me to speak up and act on my behalf. Since I was dealing with the physical pain of my condition, I asked myself what was something that I could do to change the direction of my overall course. I began to really feel my pain in my ovary and my response to it. At first, I realized I would push the pain away, almost like if I could resist or ignore it then it would go away (this tactic also applied to other areas of my wellbeing and connection with self). After I started questioning and becoming intrigued by my response to push away and ignore my physical self, I began to shift my relationship with the pain. As I got curious about what the pain was telling me I began to look at places in my life that I was contributing to the pain by acting out of harmony with my body. The first place I looked was my diet because that's what I felt the more capable of tackling. When I started to get curious about why I ate what I did, when I did so, and how it made me feel I had awareness that something was not in alignment with my belief that our bodies are innately made to be able to adapt and heal, just as our hearts are made to forgive.

Exploring the diet and the acidity and inflammation which can contribute and cause further stress to the physical body are a piece of learning what you are adapting resiliently from and how to do so.

I want to add a note here, for some people your journey towards resiliency and vitality may call you to focus on your mental, emotional or spiritual self right now. Trust that. When you work on adapting towards a place of balance, centeredness and healing in one area you are impacting each area of your holistic being. My path began with my body which lead to diet, this may not be your journey. Yours may begin with mental health leading to self-realization. I am offering that all systems of our being are interrelated, and I ask that each of you begin the process of learning to adapt with resilience by asking yourself (your wise self) what it is that you need most at this time? Is your body calling out, your mind, social connections, or spiritual self? Whichever you are hearing loudest, use that to be a barometer of moving through this book. You will get to each section and part of yourself exactly when you are supposed to.

For most of us we can think of our dietary choices from the perspective of acidic or alkaline. Really, we can look at all of our behaviors and categorize them as acidic or alkaline. Acidity produces inflammation and stress whereas alkalinity promotes balance and harmony.

Acidity

The term acidity has typically been used to describe acidity in the body (which we will also explore). Here however, I am using it in the broader sense of the word (bitterness or sharpness in tone or causing discomfort). I am sure all of us can call upon a whole host of experiences and memories from our early lives where we were met with bitterness, reactivity and sharp reactions or maybe we were the ones acting out upon those. I would also beg to argue that maybe our diets and lifestyles would mirror those reactions. Filling ourselves with too little sleep, too much caffeine, soda or alcohol, and the interactions we had with others may have been tumultuous at best. This is not to say these are the choices and experiences we always had but

there seems to be a correlation between acidic relationships,

lifestyle behaviors, and dietary choices to our ability to

connect with our sacred and divine selves. It is almost as if,

the more that the acidity rises through our diets,

relationships, home environments, lifestyle choices the

greater the muffling to our sovereignty also increases.

Nutritional Inflammation

Nutritional stress is regularly demonstrated by our

eating patterns. We can get in ruts and can frequently make

poor nutritional choices. Our dietary patterns and choices can say a lot about our relationship to balance and self-awareness. For some of us, as we are exposed to psychosocial stressors, certain emotions or thoughts, the quality of our nutritional choices can become impacted.

When we discuss nutritional stress and inflammation, we are really talking about a series of chronic and repeated dietary choices. Inflammatory nutritional choices involve foods that are processed (really most things that come in a package), fast cheap food, and animal products. The continued reliance on these types of foods, tend to provide nutritionally depleted calories. The quality of these food choices also comes into question. The toxic load of grilled meat, sprayed vegetables, and chemical additives quickly can trigger an inflammatory reaction.

It's not that these foods eaten sparsely or on occasion are inherently bad (though they are not great). It is the reality that these are often daily choices, when done chronically, they absolutely add additional stress and inflammation to the body and contribute to preventable chronic diseases (heart, diabetes, and cancer).

There is a lot of awareness about the complication inflamed bodies can cause to our quality of life and mortality. In order to steer our ship of balance and centeredness towards vital holistic wellbeing, we are presented with several nutritional changes to make. Acting to balance the equilibrium between acidity and alkalinity is essential. We must ensure that our bodies are not too acidic. When we increase alkalinity in our diets, it reduces inflammation which means we do not carry so much internal stress upon on our bodies so that we operate better in all of the ways. Neutralizing the acidity in the diet requires a few simple steps that can be hard to implement. There are some simple hard truths.

Move as close to the ground as possible is the rule of thumb. Eat more fruits and vegetables than you think is sane (13-18 servings daily), limit or eliminate the consumption of processed and fast foods, cut refined sugars out, and limit all animal products (especially those coming from un-sustainable commercial animal feed lots).

These directives are easy to write about and read. The reality of implementing them can be harder. Our diets are like any other constant choice we make, it takes commitment to sustain and awareness to allow to evolve. Dietary choices are influenced by a variety of factors.

The more acidic our dietary patterns are from eating foods that disrupt the pH balance of our bodies, the more likely our body will respond with inflammatory markers. Our diets become acidic mostly through non-whole foods (if you can't identify what a food is made from or pronounce the ingredients, most likely your body hasn't fully evolved to be able and digest the food product). When we do this repeatedly it can cause chronic inflammation. In other words, the way we eat now is not the way we ate 100 years ago or even further back. We have completely changed the landscape of the food system. For the most part, we have come out of alignment with our connection to the land and the food provided sustainably. Our food patterns have shifted, as we forgot or stopped practicing ancestral ways of connecting with the land and adopted a faster paced life. We then became more sedentary and frequently chose foods based on convenience.

We are seeing the consequences of shifting our food system, commercialization and privatization of food, and the impacts upon land, labor and health. We have fields filled with genetically modified crops. That feature one single crop after another. You could say that we have an acidic relationship with the land. We take what we want without fully recognizing how to be responsible and give back, we lack that awareness. As we collectively made these changes with our diets and lifestyle behaviors, chronic diseases (type 2 diabetes, heart disease and cancers) have increased due to a variety of interpersonal, environmental and social reasons. The common denominator in every chronic disease is an underlying presence of inflammation. This inflammation can be provoked by acidic dietary choices and stress-dominant lifestyle. We are being asked to neutralize the stress, function at our best physiologically and adapt from a place of centeredness. Let's look at what happens to inflammation and inflammatory reactions physically when we incorporate a more alkaline nutrient diet.

Alkalinity

Alkaline relationships are ones where there is a profound sense of balance, where we are encouraged to lean into vulnerability and are supported in dismantling acidic reactions. Changing our diets and lifestyles towards ones which are more alkaline ask us to lean into neutralizing the weight and reactivity of acidity. We can change what we are drinking and eating as a means to reducing the acidic load of our nutritional choices. We can also alter the acidity in our lifestyles by increasing alkaline and balancing behaviors that include sleep, self-care, presence practices, movement and greater ease. Let us begin with returning to our connection with the land.

Plant Based Healing

The reality is that no matter if we are discussing the best ways to prevent disease, come back into our intuitive knowing, or promote a deeper sense of presence and wellness we must come back to the earth again and again. Sitting with ourselves, feeling the breeze, watching the trees, drinking clean water, eating as close to the ground as frequently as possible are ways that we ground into our bodies, higher selves and ultimately our source of vitality and wellness. These behaviors also allow us to step out of a stressed state into one based upon balance and connection.

This doesn't mean that everyone needs to become a vegan. Nor does it mean that we all need to walk around barefoot all day long. What it does mean is that the source of healing our physical bodies as much as our spiritual selves' bequests us to return to the knowing we all deeply carry in our most conscious selves. We must come back into rhythm with the world at large.

25

For me, this means I eat 95% vegan all of the time. It means I support local farmers; I frequently walk or stand barefoot on the grass and I take myself into the wood's weekly. Our ancestors once moved all of the time, they moved in accordance with the land and the seasons which dictated the relationships they had with the plants that were near to them.

Plant based healing means just as much about how many plants we are eating (which we should be eating 13-18 every single day) as it does about how we address our lifestyle and how much it is in accordance with the realm of nature, balance and connection. Plant based healing is a philosophy that asks us to tune in to how conscious we are being with our food choices, movement routines, connection to the natural world, and our connection to source energy. Source energy illuminates the energy we need in order to live every area of our life with vitality and presence.

We are seeing the results of no longer being attuned to our spiritual and ancestral knowing's. When the earth is raging from the injustices its endured, while we are dying of diseases from feeding ourselves poisons and absorbing toxins we must turn inward, to source. What we see in the macro (the environment our mother earth) is showing us the mirror of where we are no longer in rhythm with the sacredness of existence. Just as we have to attend to cleaning the rivers, quitting the factory farming of animals, and poisoning of our air; we have to attend to the internal of what are the conditions of our thoughts, are we feeding ourselves by successful and supportive work and relationships, and we cleansing ourselves of what doesn't serve?

Plant based eating has exhibited evidence of reducing circulating inflammatory markers. Most of the studies show significant changes within three weeks. Eating a plant-based diet not only helps by reducing inflammatory markers, it also aids in bolstering the immune system. Plants helps to deliver phytochemicals, vitamins and minerals which can work on a cellular level to better equip immune system responses. Medawar (2019) concluded that plant-based diets have stronger impacts upon disease status (linked with inflammation) than carnivorous diets. This doesn't mean that you can't ever eat meat again but that maybe replacing the meat with more plant-based foods (13-18 servings per day) is the most ideal.

Food is medicine. It's not just medicine in the sense that it helps to deliver the nutrients that we need to live. It is also a way to connect with Mother Earth, social health, emotions, mental wellness and source energy. Taking an Ayurvedic and Traditional Chinese medicine perspective, the more we eat fresh fruits and vegetables the greater levels of Chi (life force energy) we have circulating. This Chi not only helps with immune system function but also with mental, emotional, and spiritual well-being. This source energy is found in the foods we eat, our connection with the natural world, uplifting social interactions, and inner wellness. A plant-based diet and lifestyle is based upon balance and connection with the Earth. When we are consuming plants regularly, they are providing us with the components to increase alkalinity and reduce inflammation while also delivering high quality nutrients and energy for sacred and optimal functioning.

Phytochemicals

Plants are extremely heathy for us beyond their carbohydrates, fiber, and protein. The color compounds of fruits, vegetables and herbs are particularly important because they provide phytochemicals. These phytochemicals (color compounds) are what we know to impact inflammatory markers. The more we eat foods that are rich in these phytochemicals the more we are able to neutralize how inflamed our physical bodies are as well as deliver nutrients needed to sustain us. There are different types of phytochemicals that target different processes within the body. Each type of phytochemical are found in different families of fruits, vegetables and herbs.

Each type of phytochemical is connected with a specific color compound. The family of flavonoids has the most research on its ability to aid in the prevention of chronic diseases and delivery of immune supporting nutrients. Hozawa et. al., (2007) showed that carotenoid concentrations remained higher in those who ate fruits and vegetables regularly whereas those who consumed alcohol and smoked had lower concentrations. Carotenoids are a type of plant pigment that has implications upon health and disease prevention. They are regularly found in sweet potatoes, carrots, spinach, mangoes, apricots and tomatoes among many others. They are considered to be a type of phytochemical that is able to impact cellular and inflammatory responses in the body. The lower levels of carotenoids in circulation were indicative of inflammation, oxidative stress, and dysfunction of the endothelial lining (Hozawa et. al., 2007). You find the same trend in individuals who have lower levels of all phytochemicals. This basically just means that the body does not have enough of the phytochemicals that are known to impact inflammation and immune function. Phytochemicals have the ability to directly target inflammatory markers via the gut microbiome and through the blood stream.

Nutritionally, acidity is a common experience for most individuals in modern society. We have a plethora of foods and beverages which frequently contribute to states of internal acidity. Some of the major culprits of acidity within our diets are sodas, processed foods (anything in a package), animal diets, caffeine rich beverages, sweets, alcohol and fast foods. Basically, the whole American diet leads to a state of acidity and the issue with this is that we choose these foods daily, most often multiple times in a day.

Gut Microbiome

The gut microbiome is center stage at mitigating and controlling the amount of inflammation circulating in our physiology. What we eat will either support the presence of good bacteria or aid in destroying it. If we do not have diverse and prolific gut bacteria populations our immune system will quickly suffer and a whole host of illnesses ranging from mental, emotional, digestive and physical are quick to ensue.

For most of us, it is much easier to destroy our gut microbiome and bacterial colonies than it is to sustain and grow them. We antibiotics entering into our bodies via meat, dairy, water, and our own physical consumption. We can kill our good bacteria by overlying on sanitizing agents. We minimize the growth of the bacterial colonies by having acidic guts.

We need to be exposed to bacteria in order to build our bacterial colonies. Killing bacteria, kills both good and bad. We kill our good populations off when we take antibiotics and especially when we are not taking probiotics at the same time as the antibiotics. Eating diets that are inflammatory in their nature; filled with refined sugars, saturated and trans fats, highly processed, and chemically created all play a direct relationship in the quality of bacteria we have in our gut microbiome. Equally, eating meat that has been routinely and heavily treated with antibiotics is impactful. My point is to say, that pretty much the Standard American Diet (S.A.D) is notoriously problematic when looking at how do we increase good bacteria to support our immune systems while decreasing inflammation.

Medawar's (2019) review concluded when following a plant-based diet for a month, research participants had a decreased level of intestinal inflammation. Lower levels of intestinal inflammation can mean better responding gut microbiomes. We want our gut bacterial colonies to be healthy and thriving. The gut microbiome's health is associated a multitude of health conditions ranging from digestive to mental as well as emotional. Reducing intestinal inflammation can ease digestive symptoms while also helping with neurotransmitters and immune function. Also, as we neutralize the acidity within the gut by promoting a diverse bacterial microbiome, we aid our body in its ability to absorb nutrients. When we are more equipped to adequately absorb and utilize nutrients, our bodies become able to neutralize acidity by flushing it from the system or detoxification. We cannot adequately detoxify from acidity and inflammation from nutritional intake if we are not able to deliver the nutrients that the body needs to make itself more balanced and in a state of alkalinity (plant based diet).

The gut microbiome is significant to all areas of health. When we discuss the bacteria found within the gut, we are truly discussing prebiotic and probiotic bacterial colonies. The presence of probiotics and prebiotics help to determine not only how much inflammation is in circulation within the body but also how our mental and physical health is functioning. *Bifidobacteria, Lactobacillus, and Bacterorides* are specific strains of probiotics that impact brain and behaviors (Foster et al., 2017, p. 131). If our diets are devoid of essential prebiotics, we have a hard time creating probiotics and helping to create diverse gut microbiomes and there for optimal mental and physical wellbeing. Prebiotics are what feed probiotics. We have to consume prebiotics in order to grow our probiotic colonies. In

Stress and inflammation impact the gut-brain axis which is heavily influenced by the health of the gut microbiome. The gut-brain axis is a bi-directional communication system between the brain and the gut. Through this system gut health influences brain health and vice versa. Corticotropin-releasing hormone is a hormone which is stimulated by stress and impacts the gut brain axis by increasing intestinal permeability (Lee et al.,2015). I'm sure most of you have experienced intestinal permeability. I know that when I had been in an argument or when I was anxious about making a change or addressing an emotional issue my stomach would be the first to showcase my feelings. When we experience stressors several of us will say that our digestion is impacted, we may have diarrhea or constipation. Gastrointestinal discomfort can highlight the connect between the gut-brain but can also show us where digestion needs to be supported through gut microbiome and mind-body techniques. We will explore these techniques and steps to rebalancing your gut colonies, improve digestion and support your immune system in the section *Resiliency in Practice* towards the end of the book.

As I mentioned early on, I chose to focus on how I had come out of alignment in every area of my life by choosing to address my nutrition. I continue to feel like working with our relationship and the foods we consume open the door to explore mental, emotional, social, and spiritual health. I began to realize that just as I was ignoring my intuition and the pain in my body, I was also mostly ignoring what I was feeding myself (literally and figuratively). When I really looked at why I was eating what I was, I realized there was very much a mental and emotional component to those choices. My mental wellbeing was deeply connected to my nutritional choices as much as it was to the story behind my consumption. When I stopped connecting with my intuition, I also lost my connection to the Earth. My mental, emotional and physical wellbeing was impacted as a consequence.

The physical and nutritional inflammation and acidic interactions we may have can influence changes within all aspects of our wellbeing. The physical and nutritional choices we make can produce either acidity or alkalinity (balance), these choices impact and are influenced by our mental wellness.

Mental Inflammation

When we look at mental inflammation, in one manner, we are talking about physiological inflammation that happens in the brain. In other instances, we describe the stress that occurs mentally and how we respond to the mental programming and loops we can get stuck in. When I began analyzing my disconnection to my nutrition and the lack of movement I was participating in, I quickly realized a mental loop playing. I had epigenetic stories in my mind of making the best of things. On some level, I thought I was the most helpful to others when I was sacrificing myself. I was frequently in a state of worry, which triggered a story about the need for control to help 'normalize' the worry. These aspects were hints that I wasn't in situations or connected with myself in manners that promoted a sense of balance and wellbeing and compromised my mental health.

Understanding and reducing mental inflammation can require us to look closely at what it is in our minds. They are focused on. What are the mental patterns we witness happening in our minds repeatedly? Do those sequences of thoughts change based upon people, situations, triggers? Becoming aquatinted with our mental stressors and the thoughts and stories that accompany the stress can bring us a step closer to understanding how neurophysiology is impacted by inflammation.

Bruce Lipton said, "Each of our cells is a living entity, and the main thing that influences them is our blood. Suppose I open my eyes in the morning, and my beautiful partner is in front of me. In that case, my perception causes a release of oxytocin, dopamine, and growth hormones, all of which encourage my cells' growth and health. But if I see a saber tooth tiger, I will release stress hormones that change the cells to a protection mode. People need to realize that their thoughts are more primary than their genes because the environment, which is influenced by our thoughts, controls the genes."

Stress

The key to reducing stress is understanding where and how we experience stress. Is it a job we don't like, a relationship that makes us feel small, poor eating habits, or reactive behavior routines? No matter the cause, the place to begin is to witness where and how we are experiencing the stress reaction. What are the mental patterns and specific thoughts that accompany our actions, reactions, and belief patterns? Then we are tasked with paying attention to where in our bodies we feel the stress. The mental patterns can give us the map of further exploring how we are emotionally, physically, and spiritually experiencing stress and inflammation.

Once we become aware of our stressors, we may feel inspired or hesitant to do something about them. Sometimes we can make a quick change to resolve the stress (going to bed earlier), and sometimes they may take a while to disentangle from (leaving a bad job). No matter the length of time needed in making the change, it is essential to better equip ourselves with adapting to the stress and supporting ourselves in disengaging in the stress responses. The reality is that neutralizing the effects of stress and inflammation does not happen instantaneously. We take continual steps in the journey towards harmony, equilibrium, balance, and optimal wellbeing. It takes time and dedication to decode where we experience stress, mind, body, and spirit.

The optimal way to adapt to stress is to not minimize it or pretend it didn't happen or that it doesn't exist. Equally, it is best to not undermine ourselves with a story; that we are not aware of what we are actually aware of. We must learn to address the stress head-on and understand that stress impacts all facets of our wellbeing.

Once we witness where and how we are becoming stressed, it becomes easier to disengage from the source. Distancing ourselves, so we have more room to sit with what arises rather than going into the reaction is where the magic lies. This means we have to be aware of where we are in response and unconscious patterns (mentally, physically, socially, spiritually, emotionally). When we have the spaciousness to truly be with ourselves and what is arising, there is breathing room for new creations.

Neuro-Immune System Connection

The connection between mental health is intimately tied to the health of the immune system. Our sense of wellbeing shares a relationship with inflammatory markers. Specifically, our sense and belief of personal wellbeing bear a relationship to C-reactive protein, fibrinogen, white blood cell counts, and Interleukin-6, all of which are markers of inflammation (Fancourt & Steptoe, 2020, p. 146). These markers indicate what level of inflammation is in circulation.

They can also be seen as evidence of when we are out of alignment.

Our brain's ability to build new synapses, thoughts and behaviors (based on embodying new ideas into actions) is influenced by how much inflammation and stress we are under. Stress harms neurogenesis, as that stress lowers cell proliferation and neuroplasticity, which impact cell function and DNA sequencing (Kiyimba, 2016). Our perception of stress and stressful events plays a role in health outcomes and our experiences of these stressors. The immune system operates as a sensory organ that informs the brain about inflammation. Then the brain responds by eliciting and inflammatory responses (Kavoussi & Ross, 2007). There is a synergistic relationship between the amount of stress and the personal perception of health; the higher one thinks their stress to be and the perception that it can impact health outcomes, tend to experience the worst (Keller et al., 2012). In other words, what we think and focus on can create our experiences in the world. It just so happens that the more we are focused on our stressors and how they may impact our health, the more likely they are to become detrimental to wellbeing.

Mental demands

Disarming the stories that we have bought into and made our own requires awareness. For me, I started to pay attention to where I would go on autopilot, where I would switch into unconscious living, where I was just moving through the motions without real awareness of what my senses were acknowledging. Once I became aware of my autopilot's, I realized that there were stories at play during these times that I had stopped listening to but were always playing on repeat in the background of my experiences.

Once we become aware of the stories on repeat without our knowing, it becomes easier to dismantle them.

We get to walk down the street repeatedly and slowly learn that the stories are not the steps we take.

The mental demands we place on ourselves can, in fact, be seen as acts of violence. The way we speak internally, the demands we place on ourselves, or how we judge our behaviors or actions can be acts of harm against our sovereign selves. When we chronically experience mental stress due to unconscious thought patterns, we can become intimately involved in seeing those patterns supporting the mental stress and reactivity. Cognitive stress can include memory problems, inability to concentrate, poor judgment, seeing only the negative, feeling anxious, constant worries, irritability, short temper, agitation, inability to relax, and feeling overwhelmed, isolated, or general unhappiness (Bigham et al., 2014). Our most sovereign sense of self is one where we experience ease, a sense of purpose, creation, alignment, joyfulness, abundance, vitality, health in all senses of the world, and personal confidence.

Trauma

Any type of experienced traumatic event can produce a multitude of effects upon all tenants of wellness. Trauma breaks relation: it damages human capacities for trust, connection, mutuality (Hubl, 2020). Trauma can produce a range of emotional, mental, and physical reactions, impacting inflammatory responses. Trauma exposure may be a factor that affects inflammation (Speer et al., 2018, p 116).

Sepalla et al. (2014) suggest that breathing-based meditation can be beneficial for those suffering from trauma-syndromes because it aids in reducing the hyper-aroused state. Deep breathing helps to calm not only the mind but also the physiological reactions related to trauma responses. Any type of experienced traumatic event can produce a multitude of effects upon all tenants of wellness. Trauma can have a range of emotional, mental, and physical reactions which impact inflammatory responses. Trauma exposure may be a factor that affects inflammation (Speer et al., 2018, p 116). The reality is that trauma experiences are more common than what we would like to believe. It has been argued that every individual has experienced some form of trauma. Traumas have been described as an event or ongoing experience that impacts the perception of survival within an individual and within the brain, demonstrating the ability to change the central nervous system (Hubl, 2020, pp. 15). Equally, it is argued that almost every individual in the U.S. has inflammation. Deep breathing meditation helps support the nervous and physiological systems that govern health and wellbeing. Sepalla et al. (2014) further that breathing interventions aid in emotional regulation, allowing for trauma triggers and eudemonic wellbeing.

Deep breathing meditation can inspire self-actualization, which is vital for individuals suffering from trauma. The greater self-awareness we have of our emotional responses to situations, people, and triggers, the greater control we can potentially have over our cortisol and inflammatory marker responses as well as wellbeing. When we can lower our perception of emotional, physical, and behavioral stress symptoms (triggers), research shows we can also reduce our heart rate, engage the sympathetic nervous system and develop a more profound sense of relaxation (Bigham et al., 2014). Deep breathing meditation has the potential of disrupting the conditioned fear response to the trigger, allowing for emotional healing (Sepalla et al., 2014). Learning how to engage in deep breathing meditation is not only helpful for emotional wellness. Still, it can also reduce mental strife while reducing the effects of stress upon individuals' physiology.

Gut-Brain Connection

You know that saying about listening to your gut because it understands what your brain may not? The gut-brain connection is relatively a young phenomenon from a research standpoint, with having about twenty years' worth of research being collected. What we are becoming aware of is that the gut is considered to be the second brain. Within our gut, we produce the majority of serotonin that makes its way towards our brain. What happens within the gut is further explored when we get into physical inflammation and its relationship to nutrition. But in terms of mental inflammation, the gut microbiome impacts the gut-brain axis. Basically, the gut-brain axis is the highway that connects hormones, neurotransmitters and signaling to get back and forth between the gut and the brain. This is an essential information system. The gut-brain axis is impacted by signaling between the gastrointestinal system and the central nervous system. The gut-brain axis can contribute to the release and production of neurotransmitters which influences mental health and wellbeing. The more our body is in a state of chronic inflammation (chronically elevated inflammatory markers), the more this signaling highway's communication system can be impacted. Meditation has been found to support how we mentally respond to stress and, in turn, also shows benefits to the gut-brain axis (Househam, 2017). By learning to calm the amount of stress we perceive and the physiological inflammatory response system, we may ease how communication proceeds between the gut-brain axis. There appears to be a correlation with pro-inflammatory cytokines (proteins) that can reduce the availability of some neurotransmitters which are produced in the gut microbiome (Mechawar & Savitz, 2016). If neurotransmitters become reduced due to inflammatory proteins in circulation, mental wellbeing is likely impacted.

Mental stress can create physiological changes, which in turn can impact the gut microbiome. The gut microbiome is directly related to immune system health. Also, it aids in the production of neurotransmitters that support mental wellbeing. Our microbiomes become altered because of environmental pollutants, over-exposure to antibiotics (our own, live stalk, water), and our food choices. The more our gut microbiome becomes degraded, the more likely our immune function is likely to follow. There are immune cells that exist in the brain. When the immune system gets activated, immune cells of the brain release pro-inflammatory proteins that can impact neuroplasticity (Mechawar & Savitz, 2016, pp 5). Neuroplasticity is basically the brain's ability to change and make new synaptic connections (behaviors, responses, patterns). With a limited potential to make brain changes, it can be challenging for our lifestyle changes to stick. This is part of the challenge in adapting with resiliency. We do it physically and mentally so that our new behaviors can reflect optimal wellbeing and become part of a long-term lifestyle.

Compassion

Becoming aware of what and how we desire to change to experience balance, joyfulness, and vitality is hard work! It doesn't come easily. Often, there are relapses into relationships we know we shouldn't be in, foods that are clearly not good for us, and thought patterns that make us feel small. Breines et al. (2014) suggested cultivating a sense of self-compassion can act as a protective factor against psychosocial stress and stress-induced inflammation. The more we can be on our own sides and recognize that we are engaged in challenging and demanding work that impacts every dimension of wellbeing, we can create greater allowance in our journey and compassion for ourselves.

Self-compassion may make stressors less threatening, allowing us to be better equipped at responding from places of centered awareness (Breines et al., 2014). In what ways can you show yourself compassion today? Compassion even when you are yelling, or eating that BigMac, or listening to the negative self-talk? How can we become the practice of compassion for ourselves and others? Compassion goes beyond mindfulness in that it extends gratitude, warmth, and love for the self and others (Breines et al., 2014). Maybe beginning with a gratitude and compassion journal is a start, or perhaps it's stopping reading this second and laying your hand over your heart to feel your humanness. There are a thousand ways to practice compassion for ourselves. One of my favorite teachers, Pema Chodron, says this about compassion, "Compassion is not a relationship between the healer and the wounded. It's a relationship between equals. Only when we know our own darkness well can we be present with the darkness of others. Compassion becomes real when we recognize our shared humanity." Through recognizing the places, we struggle, we can also birth the places where we experience liberation. Compassion seems to help protect individuals by reducing stress response to stressful events and lowering interleukin-6 cytokine (inflammatory marker) responses (Breines et al., 2014). The more we are willing to become compassionate with our resiliency journey, the more our body, mind, and spirit can respond with love, peacefulness, and grace.

Love

Dr. Joe Dispenza said, "When you intentionally make the expression of love a part of your daily practice, that is feeling, receiving and giving love, not only do you boost your immune system, but you begin to understand that the more you feel love, the more you become love, and when you become the embodiment of love, you can change the world." The practice of self-love is not just a feel-good story. It literally can help rewire the brain and how our immune system can function. Exploring the stories, memories, and actions that we struggle to embrace self-love is one of the critical steps to change behaviors.

Brene Brown said: "We cultivate love when we allow our most vulnerable and powerful selves to be deeply seen and known, and when we honor the spiritual connection that grows from that offering with trust, respect, kindness, and affection. Shame, blame, disrespect, betrayal, and the withholding of affection damage the roots from which love grows. Love can only survive these injuries if they are acknowledged, healed, and rare." We must be willing to do the work of tending to our emotional wellbeing through love and compassion as much as we are willing to attend to our mental programming and patterning's.

Emotional Inflammation

When we explore the concept of emotional inflammation, I am really encouraging the reflection about what could be considered emotional stress. The relationship between moods and inflammation is casual with a possible correlation (Mechawar & Savitz, 2016). What kind of moods and emotional reactions feels inflammatory to you?

Destructive response patterns can induce emotional stress. When we feel attacked and in need, to protect ourselves, we can respond in ways that can feel inflamed. When we lean into empathy and compassion, we can tap into a different sense and understanding of ourselves, others, and emotional responses. The truth is that no matter what type of inflammation and stress we are speaking of, the reaction is the same. The more we can balance our responses, reactions, and behaviors, the more well equipped our bodies, minds, and spirits are at handling the stress and reducing inflammation.

For some of us, we commonly hold emotional stress in until we can't any longer. We may feel like we need to bottle our emotions or withhold them from certain people and situations for various reasons. How we carry our emotional stress makes an impact on our body as well as our spirit. Emotional stress can decrease the immune system's effectiveness, which is located in both the central nervous system and the peripheral nervous system, and influence neurotransmitters, neuropeptides, neurohormones, and adrenal hormones (Lee et al., 2015). Decreasing our immune system function by holding onto emotional stress or even chronically being exposed to the same kinds of emotional stressors can create acidity within our mind-body-spirit connection.

Acidity

Emotionally and mentally, we can be influenced by acidic states by getting in mental and emotional loop patterns that keep us triggered, agitated, reactive, and responding from the place of fight or flight. Our hands shake, our throat catches, and our heartbeats as our eyes narrow in what feels like we are being attacked or need to attack to respond. The common denominator with acidity is that it's something that gets returned to again and again. Most of the time, these tendencies (all of the acidity types) have some foundation in early life experiences, so by the time we are becoming aware of our journey, our responses rely on well-worn grooves that don't require much thought for them to fire. We can go on unconscious autopilot without recognizing it's happening. Surviving no sleep, packs of cigarettes, fast food, arguments, coffee, fear, and anger outbursts as if this is just what life is can become our norm. We can get comfortable there, and then we become energetically impacted by the acidity. Our body experiences chronic stress, our mind is in mental loops, our emotions and mood reflect the need to protect, and we are amiss in finding and being a state of balance.

Alkalinity

Alkaline emotions and thoughts are equally based upon a sense of balance where we can encounter inflammatory or acidic behaviors, emotional reactions, or thought patterns, but they become neutralized. You may be thinking, what the heck?! How would I neutralize the patterning of inflammation and acidity within my mental and emotional worlds? We begin by naming. Naming what it is that we are experiencing, thinking, reacting to, perceiving, and believing. Then we can start the process of diving into what is beneath.

Shame + Guilt

Brene Brown defines shame as "the intensely painful feeling or experience of believing that we are flawed and therefore unworthy of love and belonging – something we've experienced, done, or failed to do makes us unworthy of connection. Shame is much more likely to be the source of destructive, hurtful behavior than the solution or cure." In fact, self-blame and shame have been shown to increase inflammatory markers (IL-6 and lower glucorotoid inhibition) (Breines et al., 2014).

Reducing inflammation and inflammatory markers associated with stress does not mean that we just stop paying attention to those responses. Instead, we must seek to relieve negative emotions while also supporting and growing positive emotional states of love, compassion, and gratitude to offset the negative emotions' adverse health and well-being (Breines et al., 2014).

Anxiety

We can experience anxiety when we are presented with new situations. Anxiety is a normal stress reaction and can sharpen our senses in new experiences (Bigham et al.,

2014). Anxiety can be described as an emotional state. In that, you emotionally may feel uncomfortable. Anxiety can also produce physiological responses. Your heart rate quickens, and your stomach may turn, your hands could sweat, and you may feel a bit queasy. Anxiety has cognitive and emotional symptomology in that there may be apprehension, feelings of being powerless, and fear of losing control (Bigham et al., 2014). Befriending anxiety can involve breathing into the sensation and recognizing the worry that exists within the experience.

Worry

The more we associate with our worries, the more the visualizations appear in our mind with passive fears (Donaldson, 2000). Mental anxiety can impact blood flow, muscle tension, and immune system responses (Donaldson, 2000). Conversely, when we use guided imagery, meditation, self-affirmation, and intention settings, we can shift our awareness and experience of worry and anxiety. We can take a direct and more active role in self-created positive thoughts, images, responses, and beliefs. By practicing these shifts when we become aware of our mental and emotional inflammation, we are aiding ourselves in adapting with a greater sense of resiliency and empowerment.

Emotional needs

We are living through a time of immense change, both socially and interpersonally. There is a pushing and pulling occurring, asking us to do better and expand. That expansion sounds amazing, like it's going to be a walk on an easy street filled with glorious balloons and unicorns. The reality is that it is hard work—some of the hardest and gut-knocking work you have ever done.

Dr. Bruce Lipton wrote about epigenetics and the connection to the stories inherited from our families and passed down generations. The stories and beliefs range based upon what our ancestors experienced. I come from a lineage of German farmers where the stories I have housed are, "it could always be worse, just put your head down and work, or this is good enough, settle in." We hear and feel these stories throughout our lives, and some of them we align with. We take them on as if they are parts of our moral codes in life. But when we begin on our journey towards actualization, the stories can suddenly become challenged.

As we begin to look at where there is acidity and inflammation in our lives, we may witness that some of it reside in the triggers and stories we hold, the ones that are actually not ours but inherited.

We are the ones that our ancestors dreamed of, which means that the workload is ours for the choosing. We are being asked in so many ways to drop their survival stories and protection and instead cultivate vulnerability within ourselves. Emotional and mental labor requires doing the fact-finding mission of seeing where we have been housing their stories and how we have emotions and mental loops that have locked them into place. Often, this kind of work requires brave vulnerability in our willingness to meet

ourselves in the most tender places.

Social Inflammation

Have you ever had those social interactions that do

not necessarily involve a lot of talking but ultimately leave

you drained, on edge, or combative? When you walk away,

there is this moment of what the heck was that? Sometimes

we can feel that way in relationships, work environments, friendships, or social interactions. What I am describing is considered to be social stress. Now that you have those experiences in mind, have you ever had to mentally prepare yourself for those interactions before participating in them? The mental toll of social interactions can impact us in multiple ways. This psychosocial stress can be enough to chronically elicit inflammatory responses and challenges to our wellbeing. Psychosocial stress is pervasive in everyday life (Breines et al., 2014). Psychosocial stress can disturb cellular processes, increases oxidative stress, and promote inflammatory changes (Dusek, 2008). The quality of social interactions we have in our intimate relationships, friendships, workplaces, and social settings can either promote wellbeing or detract from it. Chronic social stress is associated with shorter telomeres, lower telomeres activity, decreased antioxidant and nutritional capacities and increased oxidative stress (Dusek et al., 2008). All of these factors influence our overall sense of health, wellbeing, vitality, and sovereignty. Frequent hits of inflammation through social interactions can impact us mentally, emotionally, physically, and spiritually for more extended periods than just isolated bad workdays, arguments with partners, or snappy waitresses.

Hodes et al. (0214) utilized a social stress model monitoring cytokine and chemokine profiles (inflammatory markers) after aggressor (stress) exposure for anxiety, depression, and resiliency factors. The results showed acute social stress-regulated cytokine and chemokines, but interleukin-6 (IL-6) was elevated post aggressor exposure (Hodes et al., 2014). Interleukin-6 is a known pro-inflammatory cytokine, which increases inflammation and stress responses. IL-6 was significantly elevated after exposure to an aggressor in the repeated social defeat stress model, continuing to show a negative correlation to social interaction behavior, i.e., anxiety and withdrawal (Hodes et al., 2014). The ways we are impacted by adverse social events can affect our mind, body, and spirit.

Adversity

Experiencing stressful adverse events is part of human existence. We have been living through adverse events regularly for a long time now. Just turn on the news, and there will be a testament to another negative effect impacting humanity. When we experience adversity events, there are psychological impacts (Cole et al., 2015). Experiencing adversity impacts inflammatory reactions. There is a general indication that pro-inflammation markers are increased (Cole et al., 2015). We cannot always control when we experience, witness, or get thrown into an adverse event. However, we do have the power to witness how we mentally, emotionally, spiritually, and psychically respond to these events, making all the difference in how the psychosocial stress is stored, processed, or released from our minds, bodies, and spirits.

Symptoms

The behavioral aspects of stress and inflammation can be individualized and witnessed within the collective of public wellbeing. Behaviorally, symptoms of stress can include overeating, alcoholism, drug usage, sleeping too much or too little, undereating, isolation, procrastination, neglecting responsibilities, and nervous habits (Bigham et al., 2014). We cope in a variety of ways to try and outrun the stress we are chronically exposed to. We rarely try to make friends with the stressors and try to see what it is attempting to teach us.

Fight or Flight

The fight, flight, and freeze response have been helpful from an evolutionary perspective. It has helped protect us from harmful situations and often times allows us to witness how quickly we can become triggered by situations that may be deemed stressful. However, when we go into these states chronically, because of living in stressful conditions socially, they can trigger our bodies to release inflammatory markers regularly. This continued release of inflammatory markers quickly goes from being helpful to being harmful. Psychological stress can cause fight or flight responses that can stimulate a host of inflammatory markers being released. The release of these stress hormones can disrupt the microbiota's bacteria colonies (Househam, 2017). Changes to our gut bacterial colonies impact immune and mental health. We explored the role of the gut microbiome previously, but just as a refresher, the gut-microbiome helps produce serotonin; it can help address inflammatory markers and strengthen our immune function. Managing fight, flight, and freeze and where these patterns have socially become patterns within our lives is one piece of the social inflammation puzzle.

Isolation

Isolation has been a theme for the last year of existence related to what humanity has been living through. Social isolation can be detrimental to health and wellbeing. Often, social isolation breeds loneliness. Research shows that chronic social isolation is correlated with inflammatory genes being expressed (Cole et al., 2015). We need human touch seven to eleven times throughout our days to remain in our humanness, our vulnerability, our ability to care and heal. Isolation can teach us how to become friends with ourselves, and that can be scary. If we haven't ever paid attention to what it is that we think or what the mental loops of self-talk are saying, it can take some real courage to sit with the self in a way that allows the flood gates to open. Here is where we truly see all the ways we have avoided being intimate with ourselves. We may experience social isolation at times, but it can also be seen as a healing opportunity. In most indigenous communities, there are sacred times when one is asked to remove themselves from their community's social interactions to tune into themselves more profoundly. It is believed that this personal healing strengthens the community's recovery and builds resiliency to the places that are uncomfortable to address, name, and know within ourselves and others.

Resiliency

As we become aware of how we respond to social stress, we may feel more equipped with ways to overcome psychosocial stressors, especially those that are chronically occurring. Take, for example, a lousy work environment; we may not be ready to leave it just yet, but increasing our sense of resiliency may help us get through the situation until we can go. Cultivating a sense of resiliency or grit may help combat chronic stressors' inflammatory reactions (Cole et al., 2015). As we make friends with understanding that the stressors teach us where we are not in alignment with our optimal wellbeing, we can begin the journey towards self-realization and cultivate the grit to do something about these stressors rather than become victim to them.

Social isolation and loneliness are correlated with mental fatigue and disassociation. When we feel isolated and alone, it can be hard to tune into self-love and a more profound sense of ourselves. Cultivating a mental practice that helps you embody a sense of resiliency against isolation and loneliness effectively counteracts these concerns. In fact, positive mental resiliency has the potential of outweighing the negative impacts of isolation (Cole et al., 2015). Subsequently, when we experience isolation and perceived loneliness, the physiological effects can be pretty worrisome. These feelings usually come in chronic and episodic experiences; these types of incidents can condition our bodies to get used to having higher levels of circulating inflammatory markers. In the next chapter, we will explore resiliency practices that can help combat loneliness by using guided imagery, creativity, and more profound personal work.

Social Wellbeing

Jutagir et al. (2017) noted that social wellbeing is a determinant in having lower circulating pro-inflammatory markers. In other words, the greater support we have, genuine support, where we are satisfied with the quality of connection, the better our immune system is, and the lower amount of inflammation is in circulation. Take a moment. Do you have people around you that you can confide in, inspiring, that help you be your best self? If you don't, what would these kinds of people, friends, social acquaintances, or relationships embody? How would having them in your life make you feel? When we can clarify what support would genuinely feel like, it becomes easier to see what does not fit that bill. Then we can act and attract people into our lives that can support us in the ways we deeply desire.

Adaptation

Psychosocial stress is heavily influenced by isolation, loneliness, and reactions when in fight, flight, or freeze. Behind these feelings and emotions, we often create a loop that encourages more distance and self-protection. To offset the physical, emotional inflammation and stress that goes along with being in states of distance, isolation, and loneliness, we are asked to lean into cultivating a sense of belonging.

Brene Brown said, "Because true belonging only happens when we present our authentic, imperfect selves to the world, our sense of belonging can never be greater than our level of self-acceptance." Self-acceptance feeds into self-compassion, actualization, and awareness. All of these are steps in practicing resiliency and decreasing mind-body-spirit inflammation.

Spiritual Inflammation

Meher Baba describes the path of our spiritual journey as; "the spiritual journey does not consist of arriving at a new destination where personal gains what he did not have or becomes what he was not. It consists in the dissipation of his ignorance concerning himself and life, and the gradual growth of that understanding begins with spiritual awakening. The finding of God is coming into one's own self." This journey towards coming into the self is the journey of releasing and rectifying all forms of stress and inflammation. It's the process of finding out our own sense of homeostasis, balance, and vitality.

Tesla said, "if you want to find the secrets of the universe, think in terms of energy, frequency, and vibration." We are energetic and vibrational beings. We have all experienced being depleted by relationships, work environments, meals, and thought patterns. We may physically and emotionally recognize what these experiences felt like and how inflammation is linked with these experiences. We encounter these lived experiences energetically just as much as we do mentally, emotionally, and spiritually. As our energetic being starts to weaken, we lose connection with ourselves as active beings capable of creating our lives and realities from wellness, joyfulness, and creativity. We become subdued, overcome by the acidity in our lives, and ruled by the reactivity of managing that state chronically. It is almost as if we have a kitchen that is built out of cardboard. We have a gas stove and are trying daily to caretake ourselves to the best of our ability. We know-how, and yet the kitchen keeps catching fire because, well, it's paper and flames. So, we learn to keep water nearby and know that if things get damp, we will rebuild them the same way before they burnt.

Spiritual inflammation is much harder to label and categorize. First, it requires that we all identify ourselves as spiritual beings. Dr. Wayne Dyer said, "We are not human beings in search of a spiritual experience. We are spiritual beings immersed in a human experience." This can be harder to remember when we are in the midst of an argument, job loss, sickness, or financial troubles. Yet, when we begin to challenge ourselves to see all experiences' spiritual teaching, we are given opportunities to engage with our body, mind, and spirit in a new way.

To describe spiritual inflammation, we must learn how to not solely identify ourselves as having a body and mind. We must learn to appreciate that spiritually, we all exist outside of any religious designations. When we respond, make choices, and decisions, there is an energetic and spiritual reaction outside of the physical realm. I understand that this can sound really woo-woo and hard grasp, mainly if the thought of self revolves around having a body and a mind and doing things with it. What I am asking is that you contemplate and entertain that there is a purpose for everything. Not only is there a purpose, but we are also all interconnected within that purpose. Every decision, reaction, and thought carries energetic and vibrational energy that can alter our realities. If you need visual documentation, I suggest looking at Dr. Emoto's work on water molecules and thoughts. What happens to me happens to you, and so on. The study of quantum physics tells us this is possible in multiple manners. String theory asserts that at some level, all forces, particles, interactions, and manifestations of reality are tied together as part of the same framework. We can see this in research, energy medicine surmises repeatedly. Beyond this, there is an understanding of the morphic field and its contribution to the collective consciousness. Rubert Sheldrake has written extensively about all beings' interconnectivity (plant, animals, and humans). "What you do, what you say, and what you think can influence other people by morphic resonance. There is no immoral filter in morphic resonance, which means that we have to be more careful about what we think if we are concerned about the effect we have on others." When we recognize that how we respond, think, act, believe, eat and talk bear significance beyond our mind, body, and spirit, we can become empowered to continue the ripple effect of healing for ourselves and others.

The practice of reducing spiritual inflammation means that we learn how to live, react and be in alignment mentally, emotionally, physically, nutritionally, and socially. When we practice alignment in these areas, we increase our awareness of ourselves. When we grow self-agency and self-determination, and self-actualization, we can live in greater alignment with our sovereign nature. Getting there requires radical honesty regarding where and how we are showing up to truly support our progress towards our highest self.

Symptoms

When we make choices that are out of alignment with our sovereignty, the likely assumption is that they can create a stress response. This stress response can create inflammation in the physical body. This general concept can be hard to grasp if you are not aware of what living from your sovereignty looks like. You may want to begin this process by befriending your higher self and asking in what ways it would be best for you to show up. In the next chapter, there are tools to help you increase communication with your higher self. The reality is like every section of this book. It is a practice of reducing inflammation and internal stress. We take tip-toe steps, barely inching forward some days and others, we leap. Every centimeter of movement gets us closer to a lived sense of actualization, health, and optimal wellbeing.

The challenge of active engagement

The reality is that not everyone wants to be fully conscious all the time or cultivate their intuitive knowing. It is hard work, hella hard work, and it's relentless if you choose it. All of these story's flood in about how you are crazy, how we certainly cannot be aware of what we think we are aware of, or that what we are feeling must be ours and not the result of what we are aware of. The list goes on surrounding beliefs and ways we have been conditioned to remain small and unwell in multiple senses. This breaking loose leaves you feeling vulnerable and like you don't fit in any world like you have been outed. Everyone can see that you are becoming aware of things that others do not readily speak about. The story of not fitting in becomes alive when you are going through becoming you fully. There are days where you think it will be easier to go back to no longer being aware. There will be days of isolation and a deep desire to be seen or not carry the weight of feeling everything you do.

It is hard, and it is not a quick journey. It is drawn out, there are days where you will think you have the hang of your intuition and can trust all it tells you, and then there will be days that you are cussing your knowing and thinking that it's all a farce.

Learning to cultivate and listen to my intuition is some of the most liberating work I have ever done and some of the hardest. Suddenly, I came face to face with the realization of all the places and ways I had turned off listening to my intuitive self. I had to face fully the ways that I was hiding from living my life entirely. I had to acknowledge that I was using bad relationships, poor foods, and overworking to distract me from the reality of not being true to myself or choosing my optimal wellbeing. I became acutely aware of all the ways I had silenced my intuition, and let me tell you, that clean-up process was not an overnight fix.

"The human being has a natural orientation to spirituality. Indeed, our early ancestors saw spirit in everything and as the ultimate source of everything. Almost everything done in society is mechanical or mechanistically oriented. Still, we try to bring spirituality into other areas of life on special occasions. This demonstrates a lack of coherence. Incoherence means that we are working against ourselves, wasting energy, and being counterproductive (Seaward, 2000). Are you feeling ready to stop working against yourself? Prepared to stop denying how big, how empowered, how healthy your life can truly be? Next, we explore tools to address every area of inflammation, bring awareness to it, neutralize and transform it into a state of vitality, balance, and wellbeing.

Resiliency in Practice

Research has repeatedly demonstrated that when we change our perceptions of stress and inflammatory reactions, we can shift their impacts upon our physical, mental, emotional, and spiritual wellbeing. When we can lower our perception of emotional, physical, and behavioral stress symptoms, research shows we can also reduce our heart rate, engage the sympathetic nervous system, and develop a more profound sense of relaxation (Bigham et al., 2014). This isn't just feel-good information of wishing our stressors away; it is literally altering how we perceive, react, and respond to stress that can free us from the inflammation, acidity, and energy depletion traps that they can be.

Adapting and changing our situations requires that we meet ourselves with our highest and most sovereign intentions and desires. Along that path, we will meet resistance and barriers. Often the internal barriers we encounter are related to motivation and our fears (Rhodes, 2015). Marianne Williamson says, "Our deepest fear is not that we are inadequate. Our deepest fear is that we are powerful beyond measure. It is our light, not our darkness that most frighten us. We ask ourselves, 'Who am I to be brilliant, gorgeous, talented, fabulous?' Actually, who are

you not to be? Your playing small does not serve the world.

There is nothing enlightened about shrinking so that other

people won't feel insecure around you. We are all meant to

shine, as children do. We were born to make manifest the

glory of God that is within us. It's not just in some of us; it's

in everyone. And as we let our own light shine, we

unconsciously give other people permission to do the same.

As we are liberated from our own fear, our presence

automatically liberates others."

The practice of meeting ourselves by learning to truly

accept and recognize our patterns, reactions, assumptions,

and projections; provides an avenue to cultivate acceptance,

love, resilience, and agency. It allows us to live from an

actualized, joyful and ease-filled state. Self-actualization

gives us space to learn and apply calming acceptance within

the practice of meeting ourselves to cultivate a sense of vital

wellbeing. By calming our responses via self-awareness, we

are physiologically able to calm our stress systems so that we can reduce inflammatory reactions. By reducing inflammatory responses, we can help ease the mind, body, and spirit back towards a state of homeostasis. Through peaceful embodiment, there is an improved connection, personal ownership, and autonomy over mental, emotional, and physical aspects of life (Rhodes, 2015). Cultivating a sense of self-agency over all aspects of our optimal wellness (mental, physical, social, nutritional, spiritual promotes a profound healing ability. When we can embody the knowledge that we are inherently worthy of health, wellness, joy, and optimal wellbeing, we can shift all areas of our lives. We can help cultivate positive internal and external changes in mind, body, and spirit that impact our ability to socially and behaviorally respond (Rhodes, 2015). As I said about my own story and working with thousands of other people, this journey is challenging. It is filled with potholes, stones in between your toes, and heavy lifting at times. The good news is that many tools can make the journey towards resiliency easier.

Practicing relaxation and mindfulness not only calms the mind but can also help to calm the body. The practice of mindfulness asks us to become fully aware of ourselves (mentally, physically, emotionally, spiritually) in every moment we are engaging in. The act of becoming mindfully aware of what we are eating and what responses it elicits allows us the spaciousness to realize all of the sensations and reactions that surround the act of eating. The same is true when we become mindful of washing the dishes, arguing, taking out the trash, or commuting. Conscious awareness calls us back into the present moment to befriend ourselves in all sense of the world. This act of mindfulness breaks through the auto-pilot unconscious response-based living that robs us of fully feeling vitally alive. The benefits of practicing realization responses may reduce blood pressure, heart and respiration rates, and brain regions' alterations (Dusek et al., 2008). We can rewire how our brain responds, how we experience our emotions, how our body feels simply by bringing attention repeatedly to what is arising in this present moment. The beauty of mindfulness within adapting resiliently is that it is a practice to meet yourself again and again. I once had a teacher pose this question; 'what if your life, your thoughts, your steps, your words, your interactions became a prayer; what kind of presence would you want to cultivate moment by moment so that your existence could be a walking prayer of awakening'? I have come back to that question again and again. What would it really look like if every breath, thought, bite of food, conversation could become a testament to a life filled with wellbeing, alignment, support, joy, ease, and abundance?

The path towards embodiment attunement with the messages of your body, mind, and spirit requires commitment. Tools are necessary along the way. Relaxation and mindfulness are excellent practices to instill in the journey of embodiment. They make the journey easier, but they also require awareness when we go on our auto-pilot responses systems repeatedly. Practicing relaxation responses can help offset stress's physiological impacts

(Dusek et al., 2008). As Carl Jung says, ""We meet ourselves time and again in a thousand disguises on the path of life." The practice is to continue to meet ourselves repeatedly with curiosity and compassion on how we desire to fully feel alive and well.

Resiliency

Al Siebert said, "Resiliency is something you do, more than something you have. . . You become highly resilient by continuously learning your best way of being yourself in your circumstance." When we start to process how we experience chronic stress and inflammation, we begin to become acquainted with the areas in our lives where we share these internal and external trials misalignments. From this awareness, we can make different choices about how we wish to respond to chronic stress from mind, body, and spirit wellness. Cultivating a sense of resiliency involves a sense of empowerment, connectedness, acceptance, meaning, purpose, and maintaining a sense of hope in the face of stressful events (Karren, 2014). When I began to see how I was experiencing stress and inflammation due to toxic relationships, dietary habits, lack of creativity, I became aware that there may be an opportunity to choose differently. From my awareness, I realized that I could become resilient in my career and relationships and within my mental, emotional, and physical wellbeing.

Spangler and Friedman (2015) conducted research exposing participants to mental stressors quantifying heart rate variability to understand control and resiliency factors. The study indicates that resiliency is more involved in autonomic control and mobilizing towards a goal (Spangler and Friedman, 2015). This research suggests a component and connection between resiliency beliefs and behaviors and the ability to impact emotional states. When we can set a goal of becoming aware, healthy, and conscious within all dimensions of wellbeing, we can start to build resilient patterns.

Hodes et al.'s (2014) indicated that preexisting individual differences in immune systems predict and promote stress susceptibility. This research suggests that not only are emotional and psychological conditions impacted by resiliency factors. Additionally, states of resiliency can equally affect inflammatory markers, which contribute to immune system function.

Psychological characteristics of resilience can be learned, as demonstrated by the research of Mealer, Jones, and Moss (2012). Cognitive-behavioral therapy (CBT) offers an option to build resilience characteristics. There are implications for everyone by incorporating resilience training and utilizing optimism to support personal growth.

Self -Actualization

Having a deeper sense of self and how we react is essential in mitigating reactions that may produce inflammatory markers. Basically, the more we get to know ourselves, the more precise the choice we have to respond and if we desire to do so with presence or reactivity. Self-actualization can foster a sense of resiliency and mental toughness, which can aid in perseverance in the face of stressors (Schieffer, Boughner, Coll & Christensen, 2001). Abraham Maslow proposed that self-actualization was the highest stage with his model of human development clarifying, "If you plan on being anything less than you are capable of being, you will probably be unhappy all the days of your life."

With a growing sense of connection to oneself, it becomes easier to gain autonomy over your life. Research shows that as we become more connected to understanding and befriending ourselves, we can become more embodied. In doing so, there is greater control over thoughts, emotions, movement, and behavior (Rhodes, 2015). When we can react, respond, and reflect from a place of calm acceptance. The better our internal communication becomes with our optimal healthy self, the more autonomy we have over the flow and response to life. Donaldson (2000) suggests that we may experience better immune function and better coping skills for relaxation and body function by using visualization to better understand ourselves. Can you visualize what it would look or feel like to be your best self? What are the details, the thoughts, emotions, foods, beliefs you would as this self would hold? The more we can get in touch with our future selves, the more empowered we can make the changes to bring that part of ourselves into our reality. Maybe we need to see ourselves in healthier relationships and figure out the details of what could include, or perhaps it's eating better or having less anxiety and an increased presence. No matter what angle you are addressing of coming into your embodied sense of wellbeing, being able to visualize (or write, or feel) out the details of what that version of you looks like will help bring empowerment to the change journey. Self-empowerment can contribute to self-actualization by bringing you into balance mind, body, and spirit and creating a consciousness that may aid in self-healing and self-wellness (Donaldson, 2000, pp. 126).

The more we cultivate a sense of actualizing ourselves, really getting in touch with who we are and why we do what we do, we rebuild our conscious self. The part of us involved in the dance of sacred exploration is allowed to come forward and bestow the intuitive wisdom that has been residing in us all along.

Optimization, truly operating as our best and most sovereign selves, is not something most of us have a ton of models and examples available to us. What does it really look like to live a life of profoundly interconnected vivacity with the holistic self (emotionally, spiritually, intuitively, physically, and mentally)?

The greater self-awareness we have of ourselves and our emotional responses to situations, people, and triggers, the greater control we can potentially have over our cortisol and inflammatory marker responses. When we can go online and get in an argument with any stranger over the day's events, it becomes essential to increase self-awareness so that we are aware of where our energy goes. There is a saying, 'where our attention goes, our energy flows.' Is it time for your attention and energy to start flowing back to your highest sense of health and wellbeing? If so, where can you start at this moment to gain greater awareness?

Self-awareness and self-actualization have been shown to help in reducing inflammation. The more we get to know ourselves, the emotions we experience, the thoughts we think, the things we eat and drink, how we move our bodies, and the ways we connect to our spirit self, the more capable we become at living in alignment and optimally well.

Well-Being

Having a sense of wellbeing is not only helpful in terms of becoming better acquainted with ourselves, but it is also impactful physiologically. The belief that attaining optimal wellbeing as a birthright can be further implemented through the following practices and tools. Having high levels of wellbeing can help you have a sense of your purpose and meaning in life; by accessing this inner knowledge, you can also mitigate inflammatory marker release (Cole et al., 2015).

As we cultivate a sense and belief in our ability to be well and live a life of vitality, we, in turn, not only shift our mental and emotional patterns and reactions. We are also able to reduce inflammatory markers. In fact, Fancourt and Steptoe (2020) showed that those who have a higher level of subjective wellbeing also have lower C-reactive protein rates (a marker of inflammation). Wellbeing is associated with our life satisfaction, happiness levels, and ability to experience pleasure (Fancourt & Steptoe, 2020, p. 147).

Flow

The mark of being in alignment, in equilibrium, of reaching our homeostasis space is when we are actively in the creative flow. I know there will be people who read that and say, "I am not creative!" I do not mean this in the sense of being able to hold a musical tune or paint a picture. I mean the recognition that all of life is an opportunity for creation. Every moment that we are in the act of making a choice, we are in a moment of creation. No matter how mundane the options may be, we are always in the process of creating the lives we imagine.

Creativity or recognizing that we are always able to be in a state of creation is like a muscle. The more we utilize and acknowledge our choices' power, the more we see the results of moving into a state of creative flow. As we become more aligned with creation, we can use this as a vehicle for funneling acidic reactions, emotions, and behaviors through. Creation becomes the vehicle of transmutation and liberation into a more balanced life. When we choose to walk in this knowledge, it can be easier to tap into a flow-like state, where creativity and living are unfolding with ease and joy.

Expansion

Stress makes us contract. It keeps us in a state of limitation, reaction, and system lockdown. There are not many states of expansiveness that can happen when we are in fighting stress. The inflammation rises, our vision narrows, we focus on the disruption. We are immersed in the trigger zone at this point. One small thing can have a snowball effect and quickly pummel us into the space of overwhelm and reaction. However, the aim is to create more space for our minds and bodies to come back to a state of equilibrium and peace.

Lifestyle Adaptations

In this section, we will explore various wellness practices that can aid in our ability to adapt and build resiliency.

Just like when we were making our ways through the varying types of inflammation and their impacts, there may be modalities below that resonate with you and ones that don't. Both are fine, pick up what speaks to you and let go of what doesn't. The modalities and the information will be as tools on your journey whenever you desire them. Only if they fit the job you are doing.

Making lifestyle changes that create more space for processing our stressors, how we respond to them, or what it would look like to respond differently; gives us more space and more breathing room for our highest selves to come forward. We remain humans experiencing daily stressors. Yet, we can also cultivate a more profound sense of gratitude and willingness to give ourselves the space to transcend these inherited and programmed responses.

By creating space between ourselves and reactions (physical,

mental, and emotional), we can calm the body and mind. By

practicing this space through the various tools, we may gain

a deeper understanding of self and self-awareness.

Vulnerability

"Owning our story can be hard but not nearly as

difficult as spending our lives running from it. Embracing our

vulnerabilities is risky but not nearly as dangerous as giving

up on love, belonging, and joy. These experiences make us

the most vulnerable. Only when we are brave enough to

explore the darkness will we discover the infinite power of

our light." Brene Brown

The reality is no one likes stress especially stress that

they play a role in. Maybe it's not so easy to leave a job,

family patterns, or beliefs we have been choosing for some

time. This is where we practice the role of vulnerability.

The deeper we can get to know what causes us stress and

how we respond, react, and internalize our stress responses, the greater sense of vulnerability we can adapt. Here is where we can speak the truth from a profoundly vulnerable way to transmuting the stressors. Vulnerability requires truth-telling with us about where we are out of alignment with our highest and optimal selves.

Nutritional Adaptations

When we talk about the physical body, I always use food as the door that opens us to the bigger work of emotional, mental, spiritual, and social wellbeing. Food is the thread that connects us all. As we have previously explored, reducing inflammation means focusing on alkalinity through our diets. Inflammation and acidity come into our diets through processed, fried, packaged, animal-based foods. The best way to make nutritional changes is to start swapping out items that produce inflammatory reactions. Reaching for foods filled with phytochemicals (plants) as often as possible is the best way to reduce dietary inflammation and an increase in immune function. There are specific foods that pack the most phytochemical and immune-supporting punch. These foods additionally also aid the gut microbiome. Berries (of all kinds), dark leafy greens, garlic, leeks, and onions are a great place to begin. Adding in fermented foods regularly and spices (turmeric, black pepper, cinnamon, and cayenne) can help give an additional boost to immune function and digestive health. Making dietary changes can be overwhelming, so start with quick wins, challenge yourself daily, and drink a bit more water and consume a couple more vegetables or fruits. These small changes make go a long way not only for the physical body but also for mental wellbeing.

Herbs and fungi are also a fantastic addition to our regular diets for their phytochemicals and their adaptogenic properties. Using adaptogens in our diets will decrease physiological responses to stress which support our bodies and minds. Incorporating oat straw, ashwagandha, and maca root are approachable herbs that help in our stress responses. Consuming maitake, reishi, and shitake mushrooms (to name a few) can provide not only B-Vitamins, Vitamin D, and protein but also adaptogenic and immune-supporting. We can dive deeply into the realm of nutritional interventions. I have several lectures, courses, and handouts written on the specifics of eating better. The main aim is to remove processed food, reduce low-grade animal products, increase plant-based foods, fiber, and phytochemicals daily.

Most importantly, celebrate your wins! If you never eat vegetables or fruits and start with juices and frozen veggies, that is a successful step in the right direction. Celebrate your victories no matter how small because that builds Resiliency towards making these changes part of a lifestyle. Nutrition opens the door to our physical wellbeing. Healing the gut, decreasing inflammatory dietary patterns, and becoming mindfully aware of what nutrients our body needs are half of the treatment. What would it take for you to begin eating more plants, precisely 15-20 servings of them a day? Can you envision ways to sneak them into your diet to improve your nutrition and reduce inflammation? For me, it helped when I started to imagine the foods, I was eating healing my body, my mind, and my outer circumstances (I know, it's a stretch!) I really needed to challenge myself on how I was willing to nurture myself in all the wellbeing since food was something, I was doing multiple times a day; it was the most accessible place for me to connect to for making small changes. I started small, switching out sodas for water. Choosing a veggie burger instead of a hamburger. Slowly over time, I saw that my whole diet had changed and in doing so, so had my mind, emotions, and sense of self-empowerment. Maybe food is the most accessible place for you to begin, or perhaps it's a fact that we all move.

Movement

Our ancestors were on the move. It was a rarity to be able to sit around and chill. We come from a long lineage of movers and shakers. However, now we live in social structures that have limitations upon our movement. We typically schedule our time for movement rather than see it as an intricate piece of our existence.

Movement in all forms is essential to mental, emotional, and physical wellbeing. I think it's imperative to challenge ourselves about how we move. Rather than making time to exercise, I like to challenge clients to think about all the ways they move in the day that they would typically discount. Getting the laundry, vacuuming, taking the mail out, going to the grocery, or dancing around the kitchen. These are forms of movement and are all capable of stimulating detoxification, blood sugar regulation, and emotional wellbeing. The critical factor is how intense we want to become about them.

Maybe while you are making dinner, you play your favorite song and dance like no one is watching for the song's length? Or perhaps while you are vacuuming, you are also doing leg lifts? In between commercial breaks, you try to hold a plank for the length of a commercial. The point is, we can get creative about movement. Walking does wonders for the body, so does lifting weights or going to a yoga class. No matter what kind of movement routine you are ready for, go at your own pace and keep challenging yourself to be creative about how you can spice the movement up a bit. Movement offers us an opportunity to deepen our connection to our physical vessel, become curious about what type of movement we enjoy, and explore the benefits of mind-body as we engage in more creative physical practice.

Connection

Beyond addressing how much we are moving our bodies; we have also explored changing our connection to the planet and the food we garnish from it. It was once commonplace to spend days outside, experiencing the shifts in the wind, the change in a bird's song, or the babble of a brook. Now, these things are hard to notice unless we intensely concentrate on our presence. We struggle with prioritizing presence and connection as much as we manage distraction and to-do lists. We have lost the ancestral web of connection to people, plants, animals, and the simpler ways of being. The support available to us gifts us not only a deepened connection back to the land we walk on, the work we do, the food we eat, the friends we speak with, and the things we purchase but also to our sense of self.

Aromatherapy

Aromatherapy can provide a tool to change what we are smelling and stimulate new brain patterns in response to the epigenetic stories we have been housing. Whether we are breaking old stories or writing new ones, essential oils can help us hold and set new intentions for healing and wellbeing.

Essential oils can be used as part of our rituals in returning to ourselves. We can use them to help call us back repeatedly to the intentions and clearing we have set for ourselves in a very thoughtful way.

Many blends can be handcrafted and explicitly used to your emotions, stories, reactions, and intentions. I typically use essential oils to anoint myself to aid in remembering what my choices for growth are.

Some of my favorite essential oils for use on myself and altar are black pepper, rose, cypress, frankincense, myrrh, Palo santo, and sandalwood. As soon as I smell these, I am called back again and again to myself and what it is that I desire to focus on at this time.

Additionally, essential oils can be used as a holistic health modality. They are used for a wide variety of physical and mental ailments. I strongly suggest working with a company and someone who is extensively educated on oils applications before starting down the road of using them for physical wellbeing. There is a ton of information and research coming out on the efficacy of oils related to physical maladies. Like food, it is essential to know more about where the oil came from, how it was processed, and the best way to use it.

Nonetheless, the world of aromatherapy can help mind, body, and spiritual wellbeing to reduce inflammation through multiple delivery avenues. They can also help alleviate anxiety and stress, help set intentions, bring us back to the present moment, and be an excellent tool within our self-care toolbox.

Herbs

Returning to ancestral and conscious-based knowing means that we are encouraged to return to the land. That we once again remember that the land, the water, the earth; provide the basis for all medicines. The earth is the foundation of our healing. Familiarizing ourselves with herbs and their multitude of uses not only helps to connect us back to the earth but to our own power to participate in our personal healing.

Herbs can be used to make teas, tinctures, soaps, baths, meals, and other personal care products. My favorite use of herbs is to make teas. This provides you a way of handling raw herbs and making something that can be consumed very quickly. The preference is to grow your own herbs. If you are just beginning on the journey of returning to your personal ancestral knowing, that idea may seem far-fetched. Purchasing locally grown and organic herbs is then the second best.

Like plants, herbs can be used for physical needs just as much as they can be used for emotional, mental, and spiritual exploration. We may need some herbs for a day or two and others for a month at a time. For more information about what herbs to use and when it is crucial to take an internal survey on what is coming up for you right now. What is your mind focused on, where are you having sensations in your body, are there emotions that are requesting your attention? By doing a consciousness-based scan of all the dimensions of yourself, it becomes easier to format an herbal plan to support where and how you desire to be with yourself. Herbs are individualized, just like you and I, so what we need can vary. There are a wide variety of adaptogenic herbs that are always in rotation in my house to help me counteract the experience of stress. These herbs include; milky oats, mushroom complexes, ashwagandha, eleuthero, maca root, Rhodiola, and Schisandra. There are many more and picking which works for you can be whittled down by talking to an herbalist and consulting your intuition.

When I started becoming an herbalist, my teacher told me to pick one herb that I knew I really needed and become best friends with it, so I would know all of its applications. From there, I was able to build as my needs in herbs changed. Just as my needs nutritionally and physically are different than yours, so is the need for varying herbs and essential oils. This is another reason it can help build a support system as you are processing through your journey to Resiliency. The support team can help balance social stress while also helping you apply the tools that resonate in your process.

Intuitive Ancestral Connection

Our ancestors, the origin of humanity, once lived in accordance with magic, mystery, and the sacredness of existence. We are all born out of the ancestral desire to connect. Whether we are connecting with ourselves, the earth, our communities, our families, or our ancestors, we seek to connect to a bigger story—the story of meaning to our existence.

The spirit revels in the mystery of awakening. Our consciousness desires to embody awareness. When we live in moment-to-moment presence with ourselves and the collective, we quickly see the magic that surrounds us everywhere we look. There are signs, symbols, and messages that are awaiting us daily. Still, to receive them, we must slow down according to the natural rhythm of being with ourselves and existence. Just as a plant does not bloom or a fruit ripens overnight, we are asked to deepen our relationship by noticing the minute details being so innately Intune with the synchronicities of day-to-day being.

An exercise that I love to practice is asking myself what I can hear, sense, see, feel in this second and then greet all of my answers with gratitude and acknowledgment for their contribution to my present moment self.

Guided Imagery

Our ability to change and become this new version of ourselves depends on our willingness to see ourselves as that person before we have become so. Self-actualization behaviors and attitudes can be learned, nurtured, and developed, which in turn can aid in a new perspective and self-awareness of human potentials to arise (Schieffer, Boughner, Coll, & Christensen, 2001). Guided imagery practices can help in transformation through the use of imagination. Guided imagery balances the consciousness of mind, body, and spirit, which can change the response of day-to-day experiences and impact health and wellbeing through the reduction of inflammatory markers and reactions. The research's trends hint that through the use of guided imagery, the more individuals become aware of themselves and the details of their lives, the more empowered they feel to make lifestyle changes. The practice of visualization allows individuals to experience a greater sense of connection with self while also promoting a state of relaxation, which reduces inflammation and inflammatory behavioral reactions.

Guided imagery helps induce people into a state of relaxation by calming the mind by focusing on images evoking sensory awareness (Schieffer, Boughner, Coll, & Christensen, 2001). The changes in senses and in the awareness of self-promote internal communication, which impacts the immuno-modulatory behaviors. It appears that through the use of guided imagery and active visualization, there is an increase in internal communication, which may be associated with better immune system function and increased coping skills that are pertinent for relaxation and also body functions (Donaldson, 2000).

Using guided imagery provides a psychological intervention that reduces stress and impacts the immune system's effects (Donaldson, 2000). Guided imagery practice is not only helpful for fostering the mental processing of self-actualization, but there are also physiological benefits. Guided imagery is used to reduce stress, boost the immune system, and even cope with illnesses (Trakhtenberg, 2008). The benefits of being more relaxed, centered, and transparent with our inner selves help to foster greater self-actualization, acceptance, and efficacy.

Guided imagery meditation is a psychospiritual and self-actualization method that helps stress-related and inflammatory physiological conditions (Körlin & Wrangsjö, 2002). Guided imagery can lower stress levels in psychical and mental states of wellbeing (Bigham et al., 2014). Guided imagery is a mind-body technique that effectively helps people figure out how to modify their behaviors, learn to relax, and change negative emotions (Bigham et al., 2014). The ability to see ourselves in situations in which we reply from optimal wellbeing helps engage self-actualization and our ability to take different actions.

Maack and Nolan (1999) use guided imagery in that the images help reflect personal aspects of self and help promote self-actualization. Guided imagery deepens the connection with self and can foster healing in body, mind, and spirit. Guided imagery meditation can produce effects upon the body, help individuals access their spiritual connection, buried memories and emotions, and aid in their ability to verbalize an increased sense of self (Maack & Nolan, 1999). Guided imagery is beneficial for several reasons, especially in terms of how we reduce inflammatory markers and stress effects. Guided imagery has been found to increase our self-awareness, create new possibilities, and aid in designing new ways of being involved in making personal changes (Lewandowski, Good, & Draucker, 2005).

By seeing ourselves as we wish to be, we are beginning to build the new neural networks that can help us actualize that into our lived reality. Giacobbi et al. (2017)

115

highlighted guided imagery as being impactful for stress reduction and effective in addressing health complaints, increasing physical activity, coping with stressors, problem-solving, motor function, memory, and modification to food consumption. Guided imagery can help change the sense of self, mood, improving relationships and communication, increasing awareness of feelings, gaining insight, and feeling more energized to understand the self in relation to social and environmental interactions (Maack & Nolan, 1999). Practicing seeing ourselves eating better, moving more, having healthy relationships can be a less daunting first step than changing. It can be a great place to begin the process. Maybe you have trouble seeing yourself as that person; can you think about what that reality of you would dress, smell, feel, or sound like? Attaching any form of sense to that next version of you helps build the bridge for you to begin to leap into.

Self -Care Practices

Through the process of self-actualization and building the sense of self, it becomes necessary to practice self-care. Self-care relates to our improved sense of self and ability to meet personal needs in relation to the individual and others (Rhodes, 2015). Self-care in this context is beyond taking a bath, having a cup of tea getting a massage. These are essential pieces, but ultimate self-care is the willingness to personally meet our own needs and demands in their most intimate sense of vulnerability again and again.

As we grow our self-care practices and tools, we can equally begin to develop the space for optimism. In returning to ourselves, mind, body, and spirit, we learn to heal. Through tending to ourselves through the healing process, we can access empathy. In turn, self-care can help us expand our ability to connect with others resulting in greater emotional and physical intimacy (Rhodes, 2015). Self-care within this context can include drinking water, building an altar, having a fire, lighting a candle, eating well, moving your body, journaling, and dancing wildly. Self-care takes various forms; some days, it may simply involve feeling your chest rise and fall as you breathe or giving yourself the space to take a nap. The key with self-care is that it's not another item to schedule into our days but that it's lived expression of our existence. The intentionality that meets drinking water, gardening, or sitting in the sun can determine all the ways these practices can support our whole-self healing.

Adaptations

Throughout our time together, we have been exploring how to adapt mentally, physically, emotionally, socially, and spiritually. We have discussed how inflammation and unbalance can lead us away from our fully realized selves and equally how balance and alkalinity in diet, though, and lifestyle can help adapt with resiliency. Our ability to see ourselves through these processes and meet our needs in each of these dimensions of wellbeing ultimately fosters a greater sense of self-agency and self-actualization. Self-actualization can foster a sense of Resiliency and mental toughness, which can aid in perseverance in the face of stressors (Schieffer, Boughner, Coll & Christensen, 2001). When we become more aware of how we respond to stressors, we are equipped with tools to reduce inflammatory reactions. Through self-regulation, we can free ourselves of maladaptive behaviors and ruminating thoughts which can dominate responses (Thibodeaux and Rossano, 2018). The practice of mindfulness, awareness, and meditation can impact the emotional and mental patterns, further inhibiting our immune function. The chronic release of stress hormones (through repeated exposure to mental, emotional, nutritional, and social stressors) can contribute to immune dysfunction and triggers further inflammation (Thibodeaux and Rossano, 2018). Modalities that help us learn to reduce our stress, quiet our minds, and connect with our most conscious selves ultimately not only aid in reducing inflammation. They also help support immune function through reduced stress responses while engaging us in practices to become more aware and able to change course in our mental, emotional, physical, and social responses.

Confidence

This journey is arduous, but it is worthwhile. By learning to self-regulate all systems of wellbeing, we are accepting and practicing authority over our own health and vitality. The more we become self-aware, the greater our confidence grows in standing and acting on behalf of our most sovereign and healthy self. Surrounding ourselves with statements, new beliefs, and people who support our optimal wellbeing builds confidence and Resiliency in reclaiming our best self. Believing in yourself while carrying the perception that those around you support you have been related to having lower levels of C-reactive protein (inflammatory marker) (Lee & Way, 2019). Cultivating a sense of self-agency while also increasing a belief and connection to those around you who can and support you is good for mental and emotional wellbeing. It is also beneficial in reducing inflammation, all of which are important in creating a sense of optimal wellbeing. Having the perception that there are those surrounding you and your life that you can rely on is often a predictor of health outcomes (Lee & Way, 2019). Throughout learning to adapt with Resiliency, we are really learning to reclaim our lives and live as our biggest selves. Being our biggest self is one where we lead with a sense of empowerment; we don't only think we are healthy and well, we feel so. We are willing to honor our intuition and stand on behalf of our health and wellness.

Expanding Exercises

We can begin to expand our connection to our intuition by using various tools. Connecting to our intuitive knowing is a self-care practice that fosters a greater sense of believing in your highest knowing.

During my journey, I had really lost my connection to my intuition. Truth be told, I turned it off and convinced myself that I couldn't trust myself in that manner. Learning how to listen to my intuition was a slow process because I had become so removed for so long. Some of the tools I used when I was beginning to remember that I (like all) are deeply intuitive beings are listed below. This is by no means a complete list; many others are helpful. The key with any of these modes of connecting with your intuition and expanded awareness is to give yourself time. Ultimately it is about learning to trust your knowing again. We are all intuitive; sometimes, we just lose our way of remembering it. If any of these modalities resonate with you, try them out, and if they don't speak to you, then they are not yours for the time being.

- o Tarot
- o Pendulum
- o Dream Recording
- o Therapy

- o Talking with Guides

- o Crystals

- o Meditating

- o Collage and Artistic Exploration

- o Journaling

- o Yoga

- o Nature

Flourishing

There is a lot of work required of us on multiple levels to understand and address how we are not living in a flourishing state. We must address the impacts and contributions of our mental, emotional, spiritual, physical, and social interactions. When we can understand and address each potential area that may impact our personal sense of flourishing in this life, we can make changes. Beyond the shift in our ability to actualize and embody a sense of flourishing, it appears that moving towards this embodied belief may also impact inflammation (Fancourt & Steptoe, 2020). Becoming embodied and truly present with what is arising in our mind, body, and spirit self is half of our challenge in adapting with Resiliency.

This journey asks us to clear the debris of what is in the way of feeling like we get to live in vitality, wellness, and joyfulness. This uncovering is physical as much as it is mental and spiritual. As William James said, "Seek out that particular mental attribute which makes you feel most deeply and vitally alive, along with which comes the inner voice which says, 'This is the real me,' and when you have found that attitude, follow it." I am grateful for your willingness, bravery, courage, and Resiliency for being the whisper you listen to. Thank you for choosing the journey of vivacity, resiliency, and flourishing. The world needs you. May your road be filled with ease, less inflammation, a greater sense of self, and unrestrained joyful vitality.

References

Black, D. S., & Slavich, G. M. (2016). Mindfulness meditation and the immune system: a systematic review of randomized controlled trials. *Annals of the New York Academy of Sciences, 1373* (1), 13–24. doi:10.1111/nyas.12998

Bigham, E., McDannel, L., Luciano, I., & Salgado-Lopez, G. (2014). Effect of a brief guided imagery on stress. *Biofeedback, 42*(1), 28-35.

Breines, J. G., Thoma, M. V., Gianferante, D., Hanlin, L., Chen, X., & Rohleder, N. (2014). Self-compassion as a predictor of interleukin-6 response to acute psychosocial stress. *Brain, behavior, and immunity, 37*, 109–114. https://doi.org/10.1016/j.bbi.2013.11.006

Chan, H. P., Lewis, C., & Thomas, P. S. (2010). Oxidative stress and exhaled breath analysis: a promising tool for detection of lung cancer. *Cancers, 2*(1), 32–42. https://doi.org/10.3390/cancers2010032

Cole, S. W., Levine, M. E., Arevalo, J. M., Ma, J., Weir, D. R., & Crimmins, E. M. (2015). Loneliness, eudaimonia, and the human conserved transcriptional response to adversity. *Psychoneuroendocrinology*, *62*, 11–17. https://doi.org/10.1016/j.psyneuen.2015.07.001

Dantzer, R., Cohen, S., Russo, S. J., & Dinan, T. G. (2018). Resilience and immunity. *Brain, Behavior, and Immunity, 74,* 28-42. doi://doi.org/10.1016/j.bbi.2018.08.010

Donald, J. N., Atkins, P. W. B., Parker, P. D., Christie, A. M., & Ryan, R. M. (2016). Daily stress and the benefits of mindfulness: Examining the daily and longitudinal relations between present-moment awareness and stress responses. *Journal of Research in Personality, 65,* 30-37. doi://doi.org/10.1016/j.jrp.2016.09.002

Donaldson, Vann. (2000). A Clinical Study of Visualization on Depressed White Blood Cell Count in Medical Patients. *Applied psychophysiology and biofeedback.* 25. 117-28. 10.1023/A:1009518925859

Dusek, J. A., Otu, H. H., Wohlhueter, A. L., Bhasin, M., Zerbini, L. F., Joseph, M. G., ... Libermann, T. A. (2008). Genomic counter-stress changes induced by the relaxation response. *PloS one*, *3*(7), e2576. doi:10.1371/journal.pone.0002576

Eremin, O., Walker, M. B., Simpson, E., Heys, S. D., Ah-See, A.

K., Hutcheon, A. W., . . . Walker, L. G.

(2009). Immuno-modulatory effects of relaxation

training and guided imagery in women with locally

advanced breast cancer undergoing multimodality

therapy: A randomized controlled trial.

doi://doi.org/10.1016/j.breast.2008.09.002

Fancourt, D., & Steptoe, A. (2020). The longitudinal

relationship between changes in wellbeing and

inflammatory markers: Are associations independent

of depression? *Brain, behavior, and immunity, 83,*

146–152. https://doi.org/10.1016/j.bbi.2019.10.004

Foster, J. A., Rinaman, L., & Cryan, J. F. (2017). Stress and the

gut-brain axis: Regulation by the

microbiome. *Neurobiology of Stress, 7,* 124-

136. https://doi.10.1016/j.ynstr.2017.03.001

Giacobbi, P. R., Jr, Stewart, J., Chaffee, K., Jaeschke, A. M.,

Stabler, M., & Kelley, G. A. (2017). A Scoping Review

of Health Outcomes Examined in Randomized

Controlled Trials Using Guided Imagery. *Progress in*

preventive medicine (New York, N.Y.), 2(7), e0010.

https://doi.org/10.1097/pp9.0000000000000010

Hubl, T. (2020). Healing Collective Trauma. Sounds True.

Hodes, G. E., Pfau, M. L., Leboeuf, M., Golden, S. A., Christoffel, D. J., Bregman, D., ... Russo, S. J. (2014). Individual differences in the peripheral immune system promote resilience versus susceptibility to social stress. *Proceedings of the National Academy of Sciences of the United States of America, 111* (45), 16136–16141. doi:10.1073/pnas.1415191111

Househam, A. M., Peterson, C. T., Mills, P. J., & Chopra, D. (2017). The effects of stress and meditation on the immune system, human microbiota, and epigenetics. *Adv Mind Body Med, 31*(4), 10-25.

Hozawa, A., Jacobs Jr, D. R., Steffes, M. W., Gross, M. D., Steffen, L. M., & Lee, D. H. (2007). Relationships of circulating carotenoid concentrations with several markers of inflammation, oxidative stress, and endothelial dysfunction: the Coronary Artery Risk Development in Young Adults (CARDIA)/Young Adult Longitudinal Trends in Antioxidants (YALTA) study. *Clinical chemistry, 53*(3), 447-455.

Jutagir, D. R., Blomberg, B. B., Carver, C. S., Lechner, S. C.,
Timpano, K. R., Bouchard, L. C., Gudenkauf, L. M.,
Jacobs, J. M., Diaz, A., Lutgendorf, S. K., Cole, S. W.,
Heller, A. S., & Antoni, M. H. (2017). Social well-being
is associated with less pro-inflammatory and pro-
metastatic leukocyte gene expression in women after
surgery for breast cancer. *Breast cancer research and
treatment*, *165*(1), 169–180.
https://doi.org/10.1007/s10549-017-4316-3

Karren, K. J., Smith, L., Gordon, K. J., & Frandsen, K. J. (2014).
Mind/body health: The effects of attitudes,
emotions, and relationships, 5th edition. San
Francisco, CA: Pearson. Part I The Mind/Body
Connection.

Kavoussi, B., & Ross, B. E. (2007). The Neuroimmune Basis of
Anti-inflammatory Acupuncture. *Integrative Cancer
Therapies*, 251-
257.   https://doi.org/10.1177/1534735407305892

Keller, A., Litzelman, K., Wisk, L. E., Maddox, T., Cheng, E. R.,
Creswell, P. D., & Witt, W. P. (2012). Does the
perception that stress affects health matter? The
association with health and mortality. *Health
Psychology*, *31*(5), 677–684.
https://doi.org/10.1037/a0026743

Kiecolt-Glaser J. K. (2010). Stress, food, and inflammation: psychoneuroimmunology and nutrition at the cutting edge. *Psychosomatic medicine, 72*(4), 365–369. doi:10.1097/PSY.0b013e3181dbf489

Kiecolt-Glaser J. K. (2018). Marriage, divorce, and the immune system. *The American psychologist, 73*(9), 1098–1108. https://doi.org/10.1037/amp0000388

Kiyimba, N. (2016). Developmental trauma and the role of epigenetics. *Healthcare Counselling and Psychotherapy Journal,* Retrieved from https://chesterrep.openrepository.com/bitstrea m/10034/620956/10/Developmental%20trauma%20 and%20the%20role%20of%20epigenetics.pdf http:// hdl.handle.net/10034/620956

Körlin, D., & Wrangsjö, B. (2002). Treatment effects of GIM therapy. *Nordic Journal of Music Therapy, 11*(1), 3-15. doi:10.1080/08098130209478038

Lee, D. S., & Way, B. M. (2019). Perceived social support and chronic inflammation: The moderating role of self-esteem. *Health psychology : official journal of the Division of Health Psychology, American Psychological Association, 38*(6), 563–566. https://doi.org/10.1037/hea0000746

Lee, S. P., Sung, I. K., Kim, J. H., Lee, S. Y., Park, H. S., & Shim,
C. S. (2015). The effect of emotional stress and
depression on the prevalence of digestive
diseases. *Journal of neurogastroenterology and
motility*, *21*(2), 273–282.
https://doi.org/10.5056/jnm14116

Lehmann, F. S., Burri, E., & Beglinger, C. (2015). The role and
utility of faecal markers in inflammatory bowel
disease. *Therapeutic advances in
gastroenterology*, *8*(1), 23–36.
https://doi.org/10.1177/1756283X14553384

Lewandowski, W., Good, M., & Draucker, C. B.
(2005). Changes in the meaning of pain with the use
of guided imagery. *Pain Management Nursing,* 6(2),
58-67.
doi:https://doi.org/10.1016/j.pmn.2005.01.002

Long, J., Briggs, M., Long, A. & Astin, F. (2016) Starting
where I am: a grounded theory exploration of
mindfulness as a facilitator of transition in living with
a long-term condition. *Journal of Advanced
Nursing* 72(10), 2445– 2456. doi: 10.1111/jan.12998

Ma, X., Yue, Z. Q., Gong, Z. Q., Zhang, H., Duan, N. Y., Shi, Y. T., Wei, G. X., & Li, Y. F. (2017). The Effect of Diaphragmatic Breathing on Attention, Negative Affect and Stress in Healthy Adults. *Frontiers in psychology*, *8*, 874. https://doi.org/10.3389/fpsyg.2017.00874

Maack, C., & Nolan, P. (1999). The effects of guided imagery and music therapy on reported change in normal adults. *Journal of Music Therapy*, *36*(1), 39-55

Mealer, M., Jones, J., & Moss, M. (2012). A qualitative study of resilience and posttraumatic stress disorder in United States ICU nurses. *Intensive Care Medicine*, *38*(9), 1445–1451. https://doi.org/10.1007/s00134-012-2600-6

Mechawar, N., & Savitz, J. (2016). Neuropathology of mood disorders: do we see the stigmata of inflammation?. *Translational psychiatry*, *6*(11), e946. https://doi.org/10.1038/tp.2016.212

Medawar, E., Huhn, S., Villringer, A. *et al.* The effects of plant-based diets on the body and the brain: a systematic review. *Transl Psychiatry* **9,** 226 (2019). https://doi.org/10.1038/s41398-019-0552-0

Mehrinejad, S. A., Tarsafi, M., & Rajabimoghadam, S.
(2015). Predictability of students' resiliency by their
spirituality. *Procedia Social and Behavioral Sciences,
205,* 396-400.
doi://doi.org/10.1016/j.sbspro.2015.09.024

Mezuk, B., Choi, M., DeSantis, A. S., Rapp, S. R., Diez Roux, A.
V., & Seeman, T. (2016). Loneliness, Depression, and
Inflammation: Evidence from the Multi-Ethnic Study
of Atherosclerosis. *PloS one, 11*(7), e0158056.
https://doi.org/10.1371/journal.pone.0158056

McEwen B. S. (2000). Allostasis and allostatic load:
implications for
neuropsychopharmacology. *Neuropsychopharmacolo
gy : official publication of the American College of
Neuropsychopharmacology, 22*(2), 108–124.
https://doi.org/10.1016/S0893-133X(99)00129-3

National Institutes of Health (2003). *Understanding the
immune system: How it works.* NI Publication No. 03-
5423. http://www.imgt.org/IMGTeducation/Tutorials
/ImmuneSystem/UK/the_immune_system.pdf

O'Donnell, K., Brydon, L., Wright, C. E., & Steptoe, A. (2008). *Self-esteem levels and cardiovascular and inflammatory responses to acute stress* doi:https://doi.org/10.1016/j.bbi.2008.06.012

Rhodes, A. M. (2015). *Claiming peaceful embodiment through yoga in the aftermath of trauma* doi:https://doi.org/10.1016/j.ctcp.2015.09.004

Ridout, K. K., Levandowski, M., Ridout, S. J., Gantz, L., Goonan, K., Palermo, D., Price, L. H., & Tyrka, A. R. (2018). Early life adversity and telomere length: a meta-analysis. *Molecular psychiatry, 23*(4), 858–871. https://doi.org/10.1038/mp.2017.26

Schieffer, J. L., Boughner, S. R., Coll, K. M., & Christensen, O. J. (2001). Guided imagery combined with music. *Journal of College Student Psychotherapy, 15*(3), 51-69. doi:10.1300/J035v15n03_05

Seaward, B. L. (2000). Stress and human spirituality 2000: At the cross roads of physics and metaphysics. *Applied Psychophysiology and Biofeedback, 25*(4), 241-246.

Seppala, E. M., Nitschke, J. B., Tudorascu, D. L., Hayes, A. Goldstein, M. R., Nguyen, D. T. H....& Davidson, R. J. (2014). Breathing-based meditation decreases posttraumatic stress disorder symptoms in U.S. military veterans: A randomized controlled longitudinal study. *Journal of Traumatic Stress, 27*(4), 397-405. https://doi:10.1002/jts.21936

Smith, K. J., Gavey, S., RIddell, N. E., Kontari, P., & Victor, C. (2020). *The association between loneliness, social isolation and inflammation: A systematic review and meta-analysis* doi:https://doi-org.tcsedsystem.idm.oclc.org/10.1016/j.neubiorev.2020.02.002

Speer, K., Upton, D., Semple, S., & McKune, A. (2018). Systemic low-grade inflammation in post-traumatic stress disorder: a systematic review. *Journal of inflammation research, 11*, 111–121. https://doi.org/10.2147/JIR.S155903

Thibodeaux, N., & Rossano, M. J. (2018). Meditation and immune function: The impact of stress management on the immune system. *OBM Integrative and Complementary Medicine, 3*(4). https://doi:10.21926/obm.icm.1804032

Trakhtenberg, E. C. (2008). The effects of guided imagery on the immune system: A critical review. *International Journal of Neuroscience, 118*(6), 839-855. doi:10.1080/00207450701792705

Watson, J., Jones, H. E., Banks, J., Whiting, P., Salisbury, C., & Hamilton, W. (2019). Use of multiple inflammatory marker tests in primary care: using Clinical Practice Research Datalink to evaluate accuracy. *The British journal of general practice : the journal of the Royal College of General Practitioners, 69*(684), e462–e469. https://doi.org/10.3399/bjgp19X704309

Yang, Y., Jiang, G., Zhang, P., & Fan, J. (2015). Programmed cell death and its role in inflammation. *Military Medical Research, 2*, 12. https://doi.org/10.1186/s40779-015-0039-0